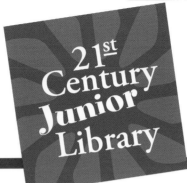

21st Century Junior Library

FARM ANIMALS
CHICKENS

by Cecilia Minden

CHERRY LAKE PUBLISHING * ANN ARBOR, MICHIGAN

Published in the United States of America by Cherry Lake Publishing
Ann Arbor, Michigan
www.cherrylakepublishing.com

Content Adviser: Laurie Rincker, Assistant Professor of Agriculture, Eastern Kentucky University

Photo Credits: Cover and page 4, ©iStockphoto.com/sansubba; cover and page 6, ©iStockphoto.com/red_moon_rise; cover and page 8, ©Shahinkia/Dreamstime.com; cover and page 10, ©Roadbully/Dreamstime.com; page 12, ©iStockphoto.com/EEI_Tony; page 14, ©iStockphoto.com/DmitryND; page 16, ©Fleyeing/Dreamstime.com; page 18, ©iStockphoto.com/dra_schwartz; page 20, ©Fozrocket/Dreamstime.com

LIBRARY OF CONGRESS CATALOGING-IN-PUBLICATION DATA
Minden, Cecilia.
 Farm animals: Chickens / by Cecilia Minden.
   p. cm.—(21st century junior library)
 Includes index.
 ISBN-13: 978-1-60279-545-7
 ISBN-10: 1-60279-545-2
 1. Chickens—Juvenile literature. I. Title. II. Title: Chickens. III. Series.
 SF487.5.M56 2010
 636.5—dc22   2009003576

Cherry Lake Publishing would like to acknowledge the work of
The Partnership for 21st Century Skills.
Please visit www.21stcenturyskills.org for more information.

CONTENTS

Some chickens are kept in barns. Others are allowed to wander outside.

Who Says Cluck?

Have you ever been to a **poultry** farm? It can get very noisy. Chickens are social animals. They like to talk to each other! What else do chickens like to do? Let's find out more about chickens.

Farmers usually collect eggs two or more times every day.

Mother Hen

Hens are female chickens. They lay one or two eggs each day. Hens leave the nest after laying eggs. This is the best time to collect the eggs. Hens may stop laying eggs if no one takes them. Hens begin **brooding** when the nest has a **clutch** of eggs.

Hatching from an egg takes a long time and is very tiring.

A mother hen takes good care of her eggs. She sits on the eggs to keep them warm. She may turn each egg over many times. She might start clucking to her chicks in their shells. She is **bonding** with her chicks.

The eggs **hatch** after about 3 weeks. Chicks hatch by pecking the shell until it cracks open.

Chicks stay close to their mother. They learn a lot from her.

The mother hen guides her chicks after they are born. She shows them how to use their **beaks**.

Chickens use their beaks like hands. Beaks help chickens eat and explore the space around them.

Make a Guess!

Chicks are born with a special bump on their beaks. It is called an egg tooth. An egg tooth is hard and sharp. It falls off soon after a chick hatches. Can you guess why a chick needs an egg tooth?

Chickens depend on farmers to provide grains to eat.

Scratching Out a Living

Chickens need plenty of food and water. They peck the ground for chicken feed and scraps. Feed can be made of corn and other grains. Chickens also like to dig up bugs to eat.

Hens need a safe spot to lay eggs. A box lined with straw or hay works best.

Foxes like to eat chickens and eggs.

Chickens need spots up off the ground to **roost** at night. A pipe or long board works well. Chickens go to their roost without being told.

Most owners lock their chickens in a **coop** at night. This helps to keep them safe from **predators**. Many animals like to eat chickens and eggs.

Have you ever heard a rooster crow? They are loud enough to wake people up in the morning.

A rooster is a male chicken. There are one or two roosters in a flock of hens. The rooster's job is to protect the rest of the chickens. Roosters are loud and tough. They will attack predators to save the chicks.

Think!

There are many uses for clean, dry eggshells. Eggshells are just big enough to hold some soil and a seed. This makes eggshells great containers for growing new plants. Be creative. Can you think of more uses for eggshells?

Experts check eggs and meat. They make sure these products are safe to eat.

Chicken Products

Commercial farms produce most of our chickens and eggs. Chickens are usually raised either for their meat or their eggs. Chickens raised for their eggs are called layers. Different chickens are raised for their meat. They are called broilers. Governments in many countries make sure chicken products are safe to eat.

Meat from chickens can be part of a healthy meal.

Chicken is a good source of **protein**. So are eggs. You can buy a whole chicken at the store. You can also buy chicken that is cut into pieces. Chicken and eggs are used in many tasty dishes. Chickens are important farm animals!

Look!

Look at the eggs in the grocery store. You will see some eggs with white shells. Other eggs have brown shells. What's the difference? The color of an egg depends on the kind of chicken it comes from.

GLOSSARY

beaks (BEEKSS) the hard, curved parts of birds' mouths

bonding (BON-deeng) forming a close relationship

brooding (BROO-deeng) sitting on eggs so they will hatch

clutch (KLUHCH) a group of eggs or chicks

commercial (kuh-MUR-shuhl) having to do with business or making money

coop (KOOP) a cage or small building for chickens

hatch (HACH) to break out of an egg and be born

poultry (POHL-tree) birds raised for their eggs or meat

predators (PRED-uh-turz) animals that hunt other animals for food

protein (PRO-teen) a substance found in all plant and animal cells

roost (ROOST) to rest or settle somewhere for the night

FIND OUT MORE

BOOKS

Huseby, Victoria. *Chicken.* Mankato, MN: Black Rabbit Books, 2009.

Nelson, Robin. *Chickens.* Minneapolis: Lerner Publications, 2009.

WEB SITES

Chicken Farmers of Canada—Be a Chicken Farmer

kids2.chicken.ca/eng/games/bacf/ bacf.html
Explore this fun activity about raising chickens

Smithsonian National Zoological Park—Kids' Farm: Chickens

nationalzoo.si.edu/Animals/ KidsFarm/InTheBarn/Chickens/ default.cfm
Find interesting facts about chickens

INDEX

ABOUT THE AUTHOR

Cecilia Minden, PhD, is a literacy consultant and author of many books for children. She lives with her family near Chapel Hill, North Carolina. Cecilia's niece Elizabeth has chickens. Elizabeth gathers fresh eggs for her family's breakfast.